AN OUTDOOR SCIENCE BOOK

SEASHORE SURPRISES

◆ ◆ ◆

ROSE WYLER
PICTURES BY STEVEN JAMES PETRUCCIO

JULIAN ⊗ MESSNER

The author and publisher thank Paul
Sieswerda of the New York Aquarium
for his helpful suggestions.

JULIAN MESSNER and colophon are
trademarks of Simon & Schuster, Inc.
Design by Malle N. Whitaker.
Manufactured in the United States of
America.

(lib.) 10 9 8 7 6 5 4 3 2 1

(pbk.) 10 9 8 7 6 5 4 3 2 1

Library of Congress Cataloging-in-
Publication Data
Wyler, Rose.
Seashore surprises / Rose Wyler;
pictures by Steven James Petruccio.
   p.   cm.—(An Outdoor science book)
Summary: Explains how waves, sand,
and pebbles form at the seashore and
describes animals, plants, and shells
which can be seen when the tide goes
out. Includes experiments and activities.
1. Seashore biology—Juvenile literature.
2. Marine invertebrates—Juvenile
literature.   [1. Seashore biology.
2. Marine animals.]
I. Petruccio, Steven, ill.   II. Title.
III. Series: Wyler, Rose. Outdoor science
book.
QH95.7.W95   1991   592.092—dc20
90-49110
CIP   AC
ISBN 0-671-69165-1 (LSB)
ISBN 0-671-69167-8 (pbk.)

The Edge of the Sea

Every trip to a beach is full of surprises—
strange shells, seaweeds, and shining pebbles.
Where did they come from, you wonder.
What animals lived in the shells?
And why are the pebbles so smooth and round?
What makes the waves?

This book will help you find answers to
your questions in the sand and water where
the sea begins.

Walk barefoot on beach sand.
It feels soft and smooth, like velvet.
Yet sand grains are bits of hard stone.
The grains once had sharp edges.
But as waves tossed them about, they rubbed
against rocks, pebbles, and each other.
The rubbing made them smooth.

Look at some sand grains with a magnifying
glass and see how round they are.
No wonder the sand feels so smooth
when you walk on it.

Pebbles, too, once had sharp edges.
The pebbles came from chunks of stone
that were rolled and tumbled by water.
The tumbling wore them down.

Bit by bit, their edges broke off,
forming sand grains.
The sand polished the stones, and in time,
they became round and silky smooth.

◆ ◆ ◆ ◆

Try to make a pebble.
Rub sandpaper against a
stone for an hour. Does
any sand form? How long
do you think it would
take to round off the
edges?

The sea is never still.
Winds push against the water
and the pushing causes waves.
While a wave moves forward, the water that
it passes through stays in place.
Watch a gull that's floating in the sea.
The gull bobs up and down on a wave,
yet it stays in the same place
as the wave moves on.

◆ ◆ ◆ ◆

Ask a swimmer to put
a beach ball on a wave.
Then watch the ball
bob up and down while
it stays in the same spot.

When a wave reaches shallow water,
the lower part of it drags across the ocean floor.
The top rolls ahead of the rest,
topples over, and breaks into foam.
Now the water in the wave moves forward.
As it moves back, it may leave shells or
other small things on the sand.

If you swim in the ocean,
you probably have tasted sea water.
It's quite salty, isn't it?
There's about a third of a teaspoonful of salt
in every cupful of sea water.
The salt is dissolved, so you can't see it.

To get salt out of sea water, put a cupful of the water in a pot. Ask an adult to help you boil it until only a few drops are left. Let them dry up and a white crust will form. The crust is salt.

Sea creatures need the salt in the water.
Nearly all sea animals die in fresh water.
But those along the sea's edge
can live out of water for a few hours
by closing up tight or hiding in damp places.

Twice a day high tide follows low tide.
Watch the water rush into the shore, and
you can tell which way the tide is going.
As the tide rises, each lap of water moves
in farther and the beach gets narrower.
As the tide goes down, the beach gets wider.

Beachcombing

Low tide is the time for beachcombing.
You will want a pail to collect things
tossed ashore during high tide.
You will want a shovel, too, to dig up
creatures in the sand.
A magnifying glass will also come in handy.

Lots of shells and seaweed lie along
the line marking the tide's highest point.
That's a good place to start exploring.

10

Beach hoppers—also called beach fleas—
hop among the seaweeds.
Catch a few hoppers and examine them.
Each has a flattened body, the color of sand.
It walks on its five front pairs of legs
and swims with the next three pairs.
The last three pairs are legs for hopping.

◆ ◆ ◆ ◆

Set a hopper on the
sand, about a foot from
some seaweed. Watch
the hopper hop toward
it. Then put the hopper
in water and see how
it swims.

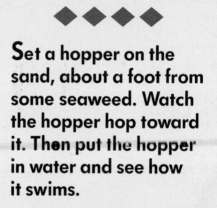
beach hopper

When the tide goes out, many creatures dig into the wet sand for safety. But you can find some of them.

If you see a jet of water squirting out of the sand, dig there and you'll find a clam. After a clam buries itself, it sticks out a part of its body that looks like a long tube with two holes.
Water carrying waste squirts out of one hole. The other sucks in new water carrying bits of food from the wet sand.

Draw a circle about a yard wide on the sand. Stand on the edge while a friend stands opposite you. Start jumping and the clams between you will start squirting.

12

All clams live between two shells
that open and close.
As they grow, new ridges form on the shells.
Some kinds of clams become as wide as eight inches;
others only get to be half an inch wide.

One kind, the razor clam, has a shell that
is long and narrow and brownish in color.
When the clam digs into sand, it leaves
a dent with two holes in it.
Drop some salt into a dent and perhaps
a live razor clam will come out.

razor-shell clam

soft-shell clam

13

Many people eat clams. So do many birds.
Some kinds of snails are clam-eaters too.
Using their rough tongues, they bore round
holes in the shells and scrape out the meat.
That's why you find lots of clam shells
with holes in them.

The moon snail may eat as many as three or
four clams a day.
It moves across the sand on its strong foot,
leaving behind a broad trail.
If you find a trail, follow it, and maybe
you'll find a moon snail.

oyster drill

moon snail

The whelk also drills holes in clams.
Although bigger than the moon snail,
the whelk eats just one clam a month.
Its shell is very pretty but whole ones
are not very common.

Sometimes egg cases with live whelks in them
are cast on the beach.
The cases are on a string.
Open a few and hundreds of perfect, tiny shells
spill out.

whelk

A snail moves slowly on a broad, flat foot.
Yet sometimes you see a surprising thing:
a shell scooting along on thin, jointed legs.
The legs belong to a crab—the hermit crab—
that has made its home in an empty snail shell.
Its front legs are claws that the hermit crab
uses to grab food.
When a hermit crab grows too big for its home,
it looks for a larger shell to move into.

◆ ◆ ◆ ◆

You can keep a hermit crab in a jar of sea water. Keep it in a cool place and feed it fish food twice a week. Take out uneaten food after an hour. As the sea water evaporates, add fresh water from the tap. Also add a slightly bigger shell that the crab can use when it grows.

hermit crab

Marsh grass is the home of the fiddler crab.
It is called a fiddler because the male has
one front claw that's bigger than the other.
This crab moves sideways.

The mole crab, or sand bug, moves backwards
through the sand.
As it digs a hole, its feelers stick out,
and so the crab can tell what is going on around it.

fiddler crab

mole crab

jingle shells

One of the prettiest shells on the beach
is the thin jingle shell.
Some jingles are golden; some are silvery.
Like clams, they live between two shells,
but they do not dig into the sand.
Each has threads that go through a hole
in the bottom shell and anchor on a rock.

By the way, if you string some jingle shells
with holes, you'll have a nice necklace.

18

The shells of scallops are beautiful, too. They are quite common on sandy beaches, but the live animals stay in the water between two shells.
They see with tiny blue eyes that stick out between the rims of their shells.

A scallop is a jerky swimmer. It opens and closes its shells, forcing out jets of water that drive it in the opposite direction. The animal has few enemies and may live five or six years.

To tell a scallop shell's age, count the ridges on the rim. A new ridge forms each year as the scallop grows.

scallop

19

Did you ever eat scallops?
If you did, you ate the muscles that open
and close the shells.

People eat oysters, too.
Oysters grow in clumps on flats, called beds,
where they can be seen at low tide.
Their shells are gray or brown outside,
and white and pearly inside.
An oyster may lay 50 million eggs a year,
but of that number only five or six grow up.
Other sea animals eat the rest.

Along the Rocks

Before you explore rocks along the shore,
attach a string to a plastic carton
and hang it around your neck.
Then your hands will be free as you poke
around the rocks.
You'll also want to wear sneakers—
wet rocks are slippery.

When the tide is going out, start at the
high water mark and work toward the sea.
Moving along, you go through different zones,
each with different kinds of living things.
Examine these creatures, then put them back
on the rocks where they live.

21

At the high tide mark, tiny black plants
cover the rocks, and so this zone
is called the black zone.
A small snail-like animal, the periwinkle,
lives here.
It creeps along with its head out of its shell
and eats by scraping tiny plants off the rocks
with its long, rough tongue.
In looking for food, it sometimes moves
to the zone below, the barnacle zone.

◆ ◆ ◆ ◆

**Watch periwinkles
move in a carton
with seaweed and
water. Do any of
them climb out?**

Full-grown barnacles stay fastened to rocks.
Each one lives inside a white shell
with its head pointing downward.
When the tide comes in, the shell opens and
the barnacle's feathery feet wave and stir bits
of food in the water toward its mouth.

◆ ◆ ◆ ◆

At low tide, build a
clay wall around some
barnacles. Pour sea
water over them. Watch
them open their shells
and wave their feet.

23

The barnacle zone is a great hunting ground.
There you'll find the curved tops of slipper shells
clinging to the rocks or to other shellfish.
The name is a good one, for the inside
of an empty shell looks like a tiny slipper.
When alive, these animals are held down
by suction, but waves often wash them ashore.

If you turn over some stones, you'll find
another clinging animal, the chiton.
The chiton has eight overlapping plates that
form a ball when the animal is picked up.
Pick one up and watch its shape change.

slipper shells

chitons

Look for limpets, too.
These animals live under cone-shaped shells.
As they scrape seaweed off rocks, they cut
grooves that become looping trails.
Each limpet makes a trail of its own.
When the tide rises, water fills the grooves
and the limpet wanders from its trail.
When the tide falls, it comes back to eat
bits of food left by the sea.

Pry up a limpet and move
it to a marked spot about
a foot from its groove.
The next day, see how far
it moved. Did it go back
to its groove?

25

Below the barnacles, you'll find mussels—
perhaps thousands of them.
Strong threads hold their dark blue shells
to the rocks.
When out of water, the shells are closed.
But when the tide comes in, they open
to take in water with bits of food.

◆ ◆ ◆ ◆

Put some mussels in a
plastic carton. Pour
seawater over them and
they'll open up as they
do when waves come in.

Little colored whelks, called winkles,
prowl among the mussels.
These animals drill holes in mussel shells
with their rough tongues and then pull out
the meat.

Waved whelks get their food in the same way.
They are somewhat larger than winkles
and live near the low tide mark.

The sea star is another enemy of the mussel.
Creeping along on tiny white tube feet,
a sea star keeps one arm lifted.
A red eye at the tip guides it.
When it finds a mussel, it drapes its arms
around the prey and pulls on it until
the mussel gets tired and opens its shells.
Then the sea star pushes out its stomach
and eats the helpless mussel.

◆ ◆ ◆ ◆

Put a live sea star
in a carton of seawater.
Turn it over to see
its tube feet. Watch
them grip the carton
as the sea star slowly
rights itself.

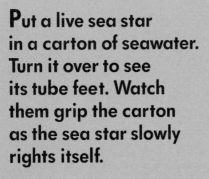

Sometimes sea stars hide under rockweed.
At low tide, rockweed lies flat, forming
a slippery brown mat.
But when they are covered by water,
the rockweed plants float and wave around.
Some kinds have air bladders that
help them stand up.

Below the rockweed you may find red seaweeds
and farther down, big brown kelp.
Both are under water most of the time,
but pieces of them sometimes break off
and wash ashore.

rockweed

irish moss

alaria

As you get near the low tide line, look for pools among the rocks.
These tide pools are underwater gardens, with draperies of seaweed on their walls.
More kinds of animals live in them than in any other part of the shore.

Some of the animals look like plants. Bristly sea urchins look like little bushes. Anemones have tentacles that look like flower petals, and velvety green sponges seem to be mats of moss.

shrimp

sea urchin

periwinkle

sea anemone

sponge

Poke around the seaweed and you'll see
sea stars gliding over them.
You'll find periwinkles with colored shells
creeping around, and you can watch tiny fish
and shrimp swimming in the clear water.

When the tide starts coming in,
it's time to head for dry ground.
All the wonders of the tide pool
will soon be hidden by the sea.

Low tide, high tide, and low tide again. Lucky you to be there, exploring and finding shells, live animals and plants, and so many wonderful surprises at the edge of the sea.